ROYAL COURT

GW00372936

Royal Court Theatre and the Festival Internacional Cervantino present

ON INSOMNIA AND MIDNIGHT

by **Edgar Chías**
translated by **David Johnston**

In association with the British Council and the Centro Cultural Helénico.

First performance at the Royal Court Jerwood Theatre Upstairs,
Sloane Square, London on 22nd September 2006.

ON INSOMNIA AND MIDNIGHT is presented as part of the International Playwrights
series, A Genesis Project, with additional support from the Anglo-Mexican Foundation, the
Mexican Embassy to the United Kingdom (through the Ministry of Foreign Affairs) and the
México Tourism Board.

ON INSOMNIA AND MIDNIGHT
A Tale to Frighten Chambermaids

by **Edgar Chías**
translated by **David Johnston**

She **Vanessa Bauche**
He **Nicholas Le Prevost**

Director **Hettie Macdonald**
Designer **Lizzie Clachan**
Lighting Designer **Rick Fisher**
Sound Designer **Paul Arditti**
Assistant Director **Simon Breden**
Casting **Lisa Makin**
Production Manager **Sue Bird**
Stage Managers **Bryony Milne, Charlotte Padgham**
Costume Supervisor **Jackie Orton**
Company Voice Work **Neil Swain**

The Royal Court and Stage Management wish to thank the following for their help with this production: Cerveceria Cuauhtemoc Moctezuma, Fiona Glascott, Robert Glennister, José Cuervo International.

THE COMPANY

Edgar Chías (writer)
Edgar Chías is a playwright, actor, theatre critic and translator, and was a member of the Royal Court Writers Group in Mexico City. A reading of On Insomnia and Midnight took place as part of Arena Mexico in January 2006 at the Royal Court. Other plays include: ¿Último Round?, Circo para bobos (Foro La Gruta, Centro Cultural Helénico); Cuando quiero llorar (Teatro Helénico, Centro Cultural Helénico); La Mirada del Sordo (Sala Miguel Covarrubias del Centro Cultural Universitario, UNAM); Familias Familiares (Oficinas del Fondo de Cultura Económica); Cuentos Chinos (Teatro Julio Jiménez Rueda, INBA); Telefonemas (Teatro La Capilla); El Cielo en la Piel (Teatro La Capilla); En las Montañas Azules (Museo de la Ciudad de Querétaro).

Paul Arditti (sound designer)
Paul has designed the sound for over 70 productions at the Royal Court since 1993. Other theatre includes: Billy Elliot (Victoria Palace); The Tempest (Tron); The Bee (Soho); Market Boy, The Permanent Way (National); Enemies (Almeida); The Crucible (Gielgud/RSC); Festen (Almeida/West End/Broadway); Tintin (Young Vic at the Barbican); Trade (RSC/Soho); As You Like It (RSC/Novello); Mary Stuart (Donmar/West End); Blood Wedding (Almeida); Sleeping Beauty (Young Vic/Barbican/Broadway); Six Pictures of Lee Miller, Just So (Chichester); The Pillowman (National/Broadway); Cruel and Tender (Young Vic/Vienna/Chichester Festival).
Awards include: 2006 Olivier Award for Best Sound Design for Billy Elliot; 2005 Drama Desk Award for Outstanding Sound Design for The Pillowman; 2004 Evening Standard Award for Best Design for Festen.

Vanessa Bauche
Theatre includes: Juan Diego (Auditorio Nacional, Mexico); Animales Insólitos (Teatro La Capilla/Teatro Casa de la Paz, Mexico); Venecia (Teatro Lídice, Mexico);

Las Cartas de Mozart (CNA/UVE, Mexico); Stabat Mater (Foro La Gruta, Mexico).
Film includes: Imitation, Las Vueltas del Citrillo, Al Otro Lado, The Three Burials for Melquiades Estrada, A Silent Love, Digna…Hasta el Ultimo Aliento, De La Calle, Piedras Verdes, Amores Perros, One Man's Hero, Un Dulce Olor a Muerte, Un Embrujo, The Mask of Zorro, Le Jour et la Nuit, Cupo Limitado, Hasta Morir, Un Año Perdido, El Patrullero.

Lizzie Clachan (designer)
For the Royal Court: Woman and Scarecrow, Ladybird.
Other theatre includes: The Ballad of Bobby Francois, The Tennis Show, Dance Bear Dance, Tropicana (Shunt); Amato Saltone (Shunt/National); Miss Julie, Gobbo (National Theatre of Scotland); Bedtime Story & The End of the Beginning (Union Theatre/Young Vic); Factory Girls (Arcola); Ether Frolics (Shunt/Sound & Fury); The American Pilot (RSC); All in the Timing (Peepolykus national tour); Moonstone (Royal Exchange).
Lizzie was a founder member of Shunt in 1998.

Rick Fisher (lighting designer)
For the Royal Court: Sugar Mummies, A Number, Far Away (and NY Theatre Workshop), My Zinc Bed, Via Dolorosa (and Broadway), The Old Neighborhood, Fair Game, Hysteria, The Changing Room, Rat in the Skull (Royal Court Classics), King Lear, Six Degrees of Separation (and Comedy Theatre), The Queen and I (and Vaudeville Theatre), Serious Money, Bloody Poetry, Three Birds Alighting on a Field, A Mouthful of Birds.
Other theatre includes: Billy Elliot, the Musical (Victoria Palace); Tin Tin (Barbican); The Bee (Soho Theatre); Jerry Springer The Opera (Cambridge); Old Times, Lobby Hero, A Boston Marriage (Donmar/New Ambassadors); A Russian in the Woods (RSC); Mother Clap's Molly House (National/Aldwych); Star Quality (Apollo);

ADDENDUM

Simon Breden (Assistant Director)
For the Royal Court: Way to Heaven
As assistant director: Tejas Verdes (Gate)
As director: The Living and the Dead
(Pinter Studio); The Pretenders; Little
Yellow Different (Gate); Slowburn
(Etcetera); Yellow Rain (Embassy); Protect
Me (Young Vic); The Bear, The Proposal
(Landor); Detour (St. Mark's Church);
Yerma; Someone Who'll Watch Over Me;
In the Burning Darkness (Burton Taylor
Studio)
As translator: Death by Love (Royal Court
International Residency); The Living and the
Dead (Gate)

Napoleon (Shaftesbury); A Winter's Tale, Albert Speer, Blue/Orange, Widowers' Houses, Flight, Death of a Salesman, Machinal (National); An Inspector Calls (National/Garrick/Aldwych/Broadway); The Hunchback of Notre Dame (Berlin).
Dance includes: Swan Lake (Sadler's Wells/ Los Angeles/Broadway), Cinderella (Piccadilly/Los Angeles).
Opera includes: Betrothal in a Monastery (Glyndebourne); Wozzeck (ROH); Fiery Angel, Turandot (Bolshoi); Peter Grimes, La Sonnambula, Clemenza di Tito, Traviata, Egyptian Helen, Wozzeck (Santa Fe); La Vestale, Verdi Requiem, Dr Ox's Experiment, Fairy Queen (ENO); Flying Dutchman (Bordeaux); Gloriana, Medea, La Boheme (Opera North).
Awards include: Olivier Award for Hysteria (Royal Court), Lady in the Dark, Chips with Everything, Machinal (National), Moonlight (Almeida); Tony Award for An Inspector Calls (Broadway).
Rick is Chairman of the Association of Lighting Designers.

David Johnston (translator)
For the Royal Court: Juan Mayorga's Way to Heaven.
Other translations include: Lope de Vega's The Dog in the Manger (RSC/Austin Shakespeare Festival, Texas); Calderón's The Painter of Dishonour (RSC); Lope de Vega's Madness in Valencia (Gate/RSC); The Gentleman from Olmedo (Gate/Watermill, Newbury); The Great Pretenders, Gil Vicente's The Boat Plays, Valle-Inclán's The Barbarous Comedies, Bohemian Lights, Vargas Llosa's The Madman of the Balconies (Gate); Divine Words (BBC Radio 3); Blood Wedding (Communicado, Bruiser); The Public (BBC); La Chunga: The Woman of Our Dreams (Lyric, Belfast).
Original work includes: El Quijote (Gate); Hambone's Day, The Shadow of the Wedding, The Priest (BBC); Dark Root, Bitter Flower (Strathclyde Theatre Group); The Poet in the City (Crescent Arts Centre, Belfast).

Nicholas Le Prevost
For the Royal Court: Blood, The Glad Hand, The Last Supper, Seven Lears, Victory, Golgo, Eastern Promise (and Mayday Festival), The Strip.
Other theatre includes: The Wild Duck (Donmar Warehouse), The Philadelphia Story (Old Vic), Insignificance (Crucible, Sheffield), Fuddy Meers (Birmingham Rep/Arts Theatre), Mozart's Impressario (Barbican), Where There's a Will (tour).
Television includes: Silent Witness, Life Begins, Poirot, Absolute Power, The Murder Room, Forty Something, My Dad's the Prime Minister, Inspector Morse, Midsomer Murders, The Borgias, Kavanagh QC, The King's Servant, The Vicar of Dibley, Up the Garden Path, Stolen.

Hettie Macdonald (director)
For the Royal Court: The Thickness of Skin, Talking in Tongues, A Jamaican Airman Forsees His Death, Young Writers Festival.
Other theatre includes: M.A.D. (Bush); Top Girls (Glasgow Citizens); Sanctuary (National); The Storm (Almeida); Beautiful Thing (Bush/Donmar/Duke of York's); The Madman of the Balconies (Gate); She Stoops to Conquer (New Kent Opera); The Yiddish Trojan Women (Soho); All my Sons (Oxford Stage Co); Three Sisters, Once In A While The Odd Thing Happens, Road, A View From the Bridge, A Doll's House, Who's Afraid of Virginia Woolf?, Deathtrap, Absent Friends, The Slicing Edge, The Nose, The Scarlet Pimpernel (Ipswich); The Party's Over (Nottingham); Brighton Beach Memoirs (Salisbury); Waterland (Shaw); A Midsummer Night's Dream (Chester); Beware of Pity (NT Studio); Leave Taking (WPT); A Pricksong for the New Leviathan (Old Red Lion); Heartgame (Soho Poly); The Normal Heart (Albery); Shamrocks and Crocodiles (Liverpool Playhouse).
Opera includes: Hey Persephone! (Almeida/ Aldeburgh Festival).
Television includes: In a Land of Plenty, Banglatown Banquet, Poirot, Dr Who.
Film includes: Beautiful Thing.

THE ENGLISH STAGE COMPANY AT THE ROYAL COURT

The English Stage Company at the Royal Court opened in 1956 as a subsidised theatre producing new British plays, international plays and some classical revivals.

The first artistic director George Devine aimed to create a writers' theatre, 'a place where the dramatist is acknowledged as the fundamental creative force in the theatre and where the play is more important than the actors, the director, the designer'. The urgent need was to find a contemporary style in which the play, the acting, direction and design are all combined. He believed that 'the battle will be a long one to continue to create the right conditions for writers to work in'.

Devine aimed to discover 'hard-hitting, uncompromising writers whose plays are stimulating, provocative and exciting'. The Royal Court production of John Osborne's Look Back in Anger in May 1956 is now seen as the decisive starting point of modern British drama and the policy created a new generation of British playwrights. The first wave included John Osborne, Arnold Wesker, John Arden, Ann Jellicoe, N F Simpson and Edward Bond. Early seasons included new international plays by Bertolt Brecht, Eugène Ionesco, Samuel Beckett and Jean-Paul Sartre.

The theatre started with the 400-seat proscenium arch Theatre Downstairs, and in 1969 opened a second theatre, the 60-seat studio Theatre Upstairs. Some productions transfer to the West End, such as My Name is Rachel Corrie, Terry Johnson's Hitchcock Blonde, Caryl Churchill's Far Away and Conor McPherson's The Weir. Recent touring productions include Sarah Kane's 4.48 Psychosis (US tour) and Ché Walker's Flesh Wound (Galway Arts Festival). The Royal Court also co-produces plays which transfer to the West End or tour internationally, such as Conor McPherson's Shining City (with Gate Theatre, Dublin), Sebastian Barry's The Steward of Christendom and Mark Ravenhill's Shopping and Fucking (with Out of Joint), Martin McDonagh's The Beauty Queen Of Leenane (with Druid), Ayub Khan Din's East is East (with Tamasha).

Since 1994 the Royal Court's artistic policy has again been vigorously directed to finding and producing a new generation of playwrights. The writers include Joe Penhall, Rebecca Prichard, Michael Wynne, Nick Grosso, Judy Upton, Meredith Oakes, Sarah Kane, Anthony Neilson, Judith Johnson, James Stock, Jez Butterworth, Marina Carr, Phyllis Nagy, Simon Block, Martin

photo: Stephen Cummiiskey

McDonagh, Mark Ravenhill, Ayub Khan Din, Tamantha Hammerschlag, Jess Walters, Ché Walker, Conor McPherson, Simon Stephens, Richard Bean, Roy Williams, Gary Mitchell, Mick Mahoney, Rebecca Gilman, Christopher Shinn, Kia Corthron, David Gieselmann, Marius von Mayenburg, David Eldridge, Leo Butler, Zinnie Harris, Grae Cleugh, Roland Schimmelpfennig, Chloe Moss, DeObia Oparei, Enda Walsh, Vassily Sigarev, the Presnyakov Brothers, Marcos Barbosa, Lucy Prebble, John Donnelly, Clare Pollard, Robin French, Elyzabeth Gregory Wilder, Rob Evans, Laura Wade, Debbie Tucker Green and Simon Farquhar. This expanded programme of new plays has been made possible through the support of A.S.K. Theater Projects and the Skirball Foundation, The Jerwood Charity, the American Friends of the Royal Court Theatre and (in 1994/5 and 1999) the National Theatre Studio.

The refurbished theatre in Sloane Square opened in February 2000, with a policy still inspired by the first artistic director George Devine. The Royal Court is an international theatre for new plays and new playwrights, and the work shapes contemporary drama in Britain and overseas.

The Royal Court's long and successful history of innovation has been built by generations of gifted and imaginative individuals. In 2006, the company celebrates its 50th Anniversary, an important landmark for the performing arts in Britain. For information on the many exciting ways you can help support the theatre, please contact the Development Department on 020 7565 5079.

INTERNATIONAL PLAYWRIGHTS AT THE ROYAL COURT

Since 1992 the Royal Court has placed a renewed emphasis on the development of international work and a creative dialogue now exists with theatre practitioners all over the world including Brazil, Cuba, France, Germany, India, Mexico, Palestine, Russia, Spain and Syria. All of these development projects are supported by the British Council and the Genesis Foundation.

The Royal Court has produced new International plays through this programme since 1997. Recent work includes My Name is Rachel Corrie, Amid the Clouds by Amir Reza Koohestani (Iran), Way to Heaven by Juan Mayorga (Spain), At the Table and Almost Nothing by Marcos Barbosa (Brazil), Push Up by Roland Schimmelpfennig (Germany), Ladybird by Vassily Sigarev (Russia) and Terrorism by the Presnyakov Brothers (Russia).

The Royal Court in Mexico

In May 2004, a new project started in collaboration with the British Council and the Centro Cultural Hélenico in Mexico City. In a workshop led by Elyse Dodgson and playwrights Simon Stephens and April De Angelis, thirteen young playwrights came from all parts of the country to take part in a writers' group, working on new plays reflecting life in contemporary Mexico. In the following 18 months, the writers continued to work on their plays with the support of British and Mexican writers, directors and actors. All of the writers completed first drafts of new plays and in December 2004 Elyse Dodgson, Simon Stephens and director Roxana Silbert returned to Mexico City to continue the development of the plays. This was followed by a third workshop with the writers in June 2005 led by Roxana Silbert, Indhu Rubasingham and Elyse Dodgson. This workshop also included a group of young directors eager to find ways of working on new plays.

As a result of this work, a week of readings of five of the plays took place at the Centro Cultural Hélenico in December 2005. During the week of 9 January ARENA MEXICO was presented at the Royal Court. Six Mexican writers were invited to London for this sell-out week which featured staged readings and other events, and was a huge success. Edgar Chías was one of the writers who came to London, and his play is produced by the Royal Court International Department.

Associate Director **Elyse Dodgson**
International Administrator **Chris James**
International Associate **Órla O'Loughlin**
Project Advisor **Circe Henestrosa**

The Genesis Foundation supports the Royal Court's International Playwrights Programme. To find and develop the next generation of professional playwrights, Genesis funds workshops in diverse countries as well as residencies at the Royal Court. The Foundation's involvement extends to productions and rehearsed readings. Genesis helps the Royal Court offer a springboard for young writers to greater public and critical attention. For more information, please visit www.genesisfoundation.org.uk

ON INSOMNIA AND MIDNIGHT is presented as part of the International Playwrights series, A Genesis Project, with additional support from the Anglo-Mexican Foundation, the Mexican Embassy to the United Kingdom (through the Ministry of Foreign Affairs) and the México Tourism Board.

AWARDS FOR
THE ROYAL COURT

Martin McDonagh won the 1996 George Devine Award, the 1996 Writers' Guild Best Fringe Play Award, the 1996 Critics' Circle Award and the 1996 Evening Standard Award for Most Promising Playwright for The Beauty Queen of Leenane. Marina Carr won the 19th Susan Smith Blackburn Prize (1996/7) for Portia Coughlan. Conor McPherson won the 1997 George Devine Award, the 1997 Critics' Circle Award and the 1997 Evening Standard Award for Most Promising Playwright for The Weir. Ayub Khan Din won the 1997 Writers' Guild Awards for Best West End Play and New Writer of the Year and the 1996 John Whiting Award for East is East (co-production with Tamasha).

Martin McDonagh's The Beauty Queen of Leenane (co-production with Druid Theatre Company) won four 1998 Tony Awards including Garry Hynes for Best Director. Eugene Ionesco's The Chairs (co-production with Theatre de Complicite) was nominated for six Tony awards. David Hare won the 1998 Time Out Live Award for Outstanding Achievement and six awards in New York including the Drama League, Drama Desk and New York Critics Circle Award for Via Dolorosa. Sarah Kane won the 1998 Arts Foundation Fellowship in Playwriting. Rebecca Prichard won the 1998 Critics' Circle Award for Most Promising Playwright for Yard Gal (co-production with Clean Break).

Conor McPherson won the 1999 Olivier Award for Best New Play for The Weir. The Royal Court won the 1999 ITI Award for Excellence in International Theatre. Sarah Kane's Cleansed was judged Best Foreign Language Play in 1999 by Theater Heute in Germany. Gary Mitchell won the 1999 Pearson Best Play Award for Trust. Rebecca Gilman was joint winner of the 1999 George Devine Award and won the 1999 Evening Standard Award for Most Promising Playwright for The Glory of Living.

In 1999, the Royal Court won the European theatre prize New Theatrical Realities, presented at Taormina Arte in Sicily, for its efforts in recent years in discovering and producing the work of young British dramatists.

Roy Williams and Gary Mitchell were joint winners of the George Devine Award 2000 for Most Promising Playwright for Lift Off and The Force of Change respectively. At the Barclays Theatre Awards 2000 presented by the TMA, Richard Wilson won the Best Director Award for David Gieselmann's Mr Kolpert and Jeremy Herbert won the Best Designer Award for Sarah Kane's 4.48 Psychosis. Gary Mitchell won the Evening Standard's Charles Wintour Award 2000 for Most Promising Playwright for The Force of Change. Stephen Jeffreys' I Just Stopped by to See the Man won an AT&T: On Stage Award 2000.

David Eldridge's Under the Blue Sky won the Time Out Live Award 2001 for Best New Play in the West End. Leo Butler won the George Devine Award 2001 for Most Promising Playwright for Redundant. Roy Williams won the Evening Standard's Charles Wintour Award 2001 for Most Promising Playwright for Clubland. Grae Cleugh won the 2001 Olivier Award for Most Promising Playwright for Fucking Games.

Richard Bean was joint winner of the George Devine Award 2002 for Most Promising Playwright for Under the Whaleback. Caryl Churchill won the 2002 Evening Standard Award for Best New Play for A Number. Vassily Sigarev won the 2002 Evening Standard Charles Wintour Award for Most Promising Playwright for Plasticine. Ian MacNeil won the 2002 Evening Standard Award for Best Design for A Number and Plasticine. Peter Gill won the 2002 Critics' Circle Award for Best New Play for The York Realist (English Touring Theatre). Ché Walker won the 2003 George Devine Award for Most Promising Playwright for Flesh Wound. Lucy Prebble won the 2003 Critics' Circle Award and the 2004 George Devine Award for Most Promising Playwright, and the TMA Theatre Award 2004 for Best New Play for The Sugar Syndrome.

Richard Bean won the 2005 Critics' Circle Award for Best New Play for Harvest. Laura Wade won the 2005 Critics' Circle Award for Most Promising Playwright and the 2005 Pearson Best Play Award for Breathing Corpses. The 2006 Whatsonstage Theatregoers' Choice Award for Best New Play was won by My Name is Rachel Corrie.

The 2005 Evening Standard Special Award was given to the Royal Court 'for making and changing theatrical history this last half century'.

ROYAL COURT BOOKSHOP

The Royal Court bookshop offers a range of contemporary plays and publications on the theory and practice of modern drama. The staff specialise in assisting with the selection of audition monologues and scenes. Royal Court playtexts from past and present productions cost £2.

The Bookshop is situated in the downstairs ROYAL COURT BAR.

Monday–Friday 3–10pm

Saturday 2.30–10pm

For information tel: 020 7565 5024

or email: bookshop@royalcourttheatre.com

PROGRAMME SUPPORTERS

The Royal Court (English Stage Company Ltd) receives its principal funding from Arts Council England, London. It is also supported financially by a wide range of private companies, charitable and public bodies, and earns the remainder of its income from the box office and its own trading activities.

The Genesis Foundation supports the Royal Court's work with International Playwrights.

Archival recordings of the Royal Court's Anniversary year are made possible by Francis Finlay.

The Skirball Foundation funds a Playwrights' Programme at the theatre. The Artistic Director's Chair is supported by a lead grant from The Peter Jay Sharp Foundation, contributing to the activities of the Artistic Director's office. Over the past nine years the BBC has supported the Gerald Chapman Fund for directors.

The Jerwood Charity supports new plays by new playwrights through the Jerwood New Playwrights series.

ROYAL COURT
DEVELOPMENT BOARD
Tamara Ingram (Chair)
Jonathan Cameron
(Vice Chair)
Timothy Burrill
Anthony Burton
Jonathan Caplan QC
Sindy Caplan
Gavin Casey FCA
Mark Crowdy
Cas Donald
Celeste Fenichel
Joseph Fiennes
Amanda Foreman
Gavin Neath
Michael Potter
Kadee Robbins
Mark Robinson
William Russell
James L Tanner

PUBLIC FUNDING
Arts Council England,
London
British Council
London Challenge
Royal Borough of
Kensington & Chelsea

TRUSTS AND
FOUNDATIONS
The ADAPT Trust
American Friends of the
Royal Court Theatre
Gerald Chapman Fund
Columbia Foundation
The Sidney & Elizabeth
Corob Charitable Trust
Cowley Charitable Trust
The Dorset Foundation
The Ronald Duncan
Literary Foundation
Earls Court and Olympia
Charitable Trust
The Foundation for Sport
and the Arts
The Foyle Foundation
Francis Finlay
The Garfield Weston
Foundation
Genesis Foundation
Jerwood Charity
Lloyds TSB Foundation for
England and Wales
Lynn Foundation
John Lyon's Charity

The Magowan Family
Foundation
The Laura Pels Foundation
The Peggy Ramsay
Foundation
The Rayne Foundation
Rose Foundation
The Royal Victoria Hall
Foundation
The Peter Jay Sharp
Foundation
Skirball Foundation
Wates Foundation
Michael J Zamkow &
Sue E Berman Charitable
Trust

50TH ANNIVERSARY
PROGRAMME SPONSOR
Coutts & Co

SPONSORS
Aviva Plc
BBC
Cadogan Hotel
City Inn
Dom Pérignon
Doughty Street Chambers
dunhill
Giorgio Armani
Links of London
John Malkovich/Uncle
Kimono
Pemberton Greenish
Simons Muirhead & Burton
Smythson of Bond Street
Vanity Fair
White Light

CORPORATE
BENEFACTORS
Insinger de Beaufort
Merrill Lynch

BUSINESS AND MEDIA
MEMBERS
AKA
Bloomsbury
Columbia Tristar Films
(UK)
Digby Trout Restaurants
Grey London
The Henley Centre
Lazard
Peter Jones
Slaughter and May

PRODUCTION SYNDICATE
Anonymous
Dianne & Michael Bienes
Ms Kay Ellen Consolver
Mrs Philip Donald
John Garfield
Peter & Edna Goldstein
Richard & Robin
Landsberger
Daisy Prince
Kadee Robbins
William & Hilary Russell
Kay Hartenstein Saatchi
Jon & NoraLee Sedmak
Ian & Carol Sellars

INDIVIDUAL MEMBERS
Patrons
Anonymous
Dr Bettina Bahlsen
Katie Bradford
Marcus J Burton & Dr M F
Ozbilgin
Mr & Mrs Philip Donald
Tom & Simone Fenton
Daniel & Joanna Friel
John Garfield
Lady Grabiner
Charles & Elizabeth Handy
Jack & Linda Keenan
Pawel & Sarah Kisielewski
Deborah & Stephen
Marquardt
Duncan Matthews QC
Jill & Paul Ruddock
Ian & Carol Sellars
Jan & Michael Topham
Richard Wilson OBE

Benefactors
Anonymous
Martha Allfrey
Amanda Attard-Manché
Varian Ayers & Gary
Knisely
John & Anoushka Ayton
Mr & Mrs Gavin Casey
Sindy & Jonathan Caplan
Jeremy Conway & Nicola
Van Gelder
Robyn Durie
Hugo Eddis
Joachim Fleury
Beverley Gee
Sue and Don Guiney
Sam & Caroline Haubold
Tamara Ingram

David Juxon
David Kaskell &
Christopher Teano
Peter & Maria Kellner
Larry & Peggy Levy
Barbara Minto
Mr & Mrs Richard Pilosof
Elaine Potter
Anthony Simpson
Brian D Smith
Sue Stapely
Sir Robert & Lady Wilson
Nick Wheeler
Sir Mark & Lady Wrightson

Associates
Act IV
Anonymous
Jeffrey Archer
Brian Boylan
Alan Brodie
Ossi & Paul Burger
Clive & Helena Butler
Gaynor Buxton
Lady Cazalet
Carole & Neville Conrad
Margaret Cowper
Andrew Cryer
Linda & Ronald F. Daitz
Zoë Dominic
Kim Dunn
Celeste Fenichel
Charlotte & Nick Fraser
Gillian Frumkin
Sara Galbraith
Jacqueline & Jonathan
Gestetner
Vivien Goodwin
David & Suzie Hyman
Mrs Ellen Josefowitz
Colette & Peter Levy
Mr Watcyn Lewis
David Marks
Nicola McFarland
Gavin & Ann Neath
Janet & Michael Orr
S. Osman
Pauline Pinder
William Poeton CBE &
Barbara Poeton
Jeremy Priestley
Beverley Rider
John Ritchie
Lois Sieff OBE
Gail Steele
Will Turner
Anthony Wigram

ROYAL COURT
SLOANE SQUARE

2 – 25 November
Jerwood Theatre Upstairs

SCENES FROM THE BACK OF BEYOND
by Meredith Oakes

direction **Annie Castledine**
design **Jon Bausor**
lighting design **Johanna Town**
sound **Emma Laxton**

Bill is sustained by his deep sense of a wider culture and an improving world. The only thing the human race needs to do is learn. When he meets a person who embodies this idea, he naturally likes them. Especially if his wife doesn't.

Set at the end of the 1950s, SCENES FROM THE BACK OF BEYOND explores the comfort, hopes and fragility of family life in a new Sydney suburb.

10 November – 22 December
Jerwood Theatre Downstairs

DRUNK ENOUGH TO SAY I LOVE YOU?
by Caryl Churchill

direction **James Macdonald**
design **Eugene Lee**
lighting design **Peter Mumford**
sound **Ian Dickinson**
music **Matthew Herbert**

Jack would do anything for Sam. Sam would do anything.

Caryl Churchill's new play receives its world premiere at the Royal Court Theatre this autumn. Her previous plays for the Royal Court include A Number, Far Away, Blue Heart, This is a Chair and Top Girls.

Supported by an anonymous donor.

BOX OFFICE 020 7565 5000

BOOK ONLINE

www.royalcourttheatre.com

FOR THE ROYAL COURT

We've always been happy to be less famous than our clients

Throughout our long history, Coutts has always been happy to be less famous than our clients. Clients such as Sir Henry Irving, Phineas Barnum, Bram Stoker, Charles Dickens and Frédéric Chopin to name but a few.

Coutts has a long and rich association with the performing arts, and we are still privileged to have many individuals from this arena amongst our clients. As a leading sponsor of the performing arts, Coutts is pleased and proud to support the Royal Court.

For more information about Coutts, call us on 020 7753 1851 or visit our website www.coutts.com

Sir Henry Irving was considered to be one of the greatest actors of his day. He played a wide range of Shakespearean roles and was a good friend of Thomas Coutts' granddaughter.

Bath, Birmingham, Bournemouth, Bristol, Cambridge, Cardiff, Eton, Guildford, Hampshire, Leeds, Liverpool, London, Manchester, Newcastle upon Tyne, Nottingham, Oxford, Tunbridge Wells.
CALLS MAY BE RECORDED

Coutts

Edgar Chías

ON INSOMNIA AND MIDNIGHT

A Tale to Frighten Chambermaids

TRANSLATED BY DAVID JOHNSTON

OBERON BOOKS
LONDON

First published in 2006 by Oberon Books Ltd.
521 Caledonian Road, London N7 9RH
Tel: 020 7607 3637 / Fax: 020 7607 3629
e-mail: info@oberonbooks.com
www.oberonbooks.com

A catalogue record for this book is available from the British Library.

ISBN: 1 84002 696 0

Cover photograph by Stephen Cummiskey

Printed in Great Britain by Antony Rowe Ltd, Chippenham.

for Beatriz and Miranda

Edgar Chías and David Johnston would like to thank the following:
Luis Mario Moncada, Elyse Dodgson, the British Council,
the Teatro Helénico, Hettie Macdonald, Nicholas Le Prevost,
Vanessa Bauche, and the team at the Royal Court.

Characters

HE

SHE

Notes

The action takes place in the bedroom of a large hotel in a provincial city.

The space is intimate and estranging. Estranging, because nobody who occupies it really belongs there; these are people in transit. Intimate, because we can only show our darkest depths, our weakness and our tenderness, the illuminations of our doubt and the capriciousness of our love, when we share that space with someone who is also alone.

HE is a man growing old, or at least he thinks he is. He feels ill. He probably is. But what he is suffering from is the decline of an intelligence that is implacable with all things, including with himself.

SHE is young, probably pretty, almost beautiful perhaps. She is not quick to understand. Indeed, she is ingenuous, even cruel: but vital.

The moment, like all moments, is a time out of time – although it is worth saying that there are gaps between the unfolding of these moments, periods of time in which something has happened and all that is left for us are its residue or its effects.

Light and shadow are fundamental elements, as are silence and looks.

Je m'suis fait tout p'tit devant une poupée
Qui ferm'les yeux quand on la couche.
Je m'suis fait tout p'tit devant une poupée
Qui fait maman quand on la touche.

– George Brassens

1

The only light comes through the door, which is lying ajar. SHE's standing with her back to him, holding a glass containing brandy. HE's sitting in the shadows, watching without being seen.

SHE: Nobody saw him. And nobody's seen him since.

HE: What do the papers say?

SHE: Not much. Nothing new. Just that she threw herself into the river. The girl, she threw herself in. That's what they say.

HE: Nothing else.

SHE: No.

HE: No photo of him?

SHE: No.

HE: All right. Shall we start?

   Pause.

SHE: Can I turn on the light?

HE: What's the matter…? It's like you were frightened. Is that what it is? Are you?

SHE: I'm not frightened, no. It's…different.

HE: Different, how?

SHE: I don't know, because I don't know how to say it. Things feel…complicated. Maybe I shouldn't be here.

HE: But you are here.

SHE: Yes.

HE: Because you're young. Everything always feels complicated, but it passes. It'll pass.

SHE: The light. Do you mind? I'd like to be able to see. That's all. Just that I'd like to be able to. I think it would help.

HE: You said that yesterday too.

SHE: I'd like to have been able to see yesterday, and I'd like to be able to today.

HE: Would you rather go?

SHE: I didn't say that.

HE: Do you want to stay then?

SHE: I didn't say that either.

HE: You can turn round a bit.

Pause.

SHE: Like that?

HE: Yes. Come closer.

SHE: Here?

HE: Yes. Now take a deep breath. You're starting to make me feel nervous.

SHE: So can I turn on the light? It's just that the shadows…

HE: Close the door then.

SHE: There'd be even less light.

HE: There'd be less shadows too.

SHE: No. It's okay like this.

HE: Let's start. Tell me something.

SHE: It's getting late.

HE: But you're here now.

SHE moves towards the door.

Stay still. Just as you are. Now relax. Tell me.

SHE: I don't know what to tell you.

HE: Tell me the same thing…

HE is racked by a sudden cough.

SHE: Are you all right? Do you need anything?

HE: I don't need anything.

SHE: I could turn on the light…

HE: You've got lovely legs…strong…sturdy legs.

SHE: How do you know?

HE: Just tell me the same thing as yesterday. I don't need anything. I just want to listen.

SHE: All right. But don't look at me. Don't. Please.

HE: I'll try not to. But I can't promise.

Pause.

SHE: Reverend Mother didn't like me.

HE: Reverend Mother was an idiot. All mothers are. How could she not like you?

SHE: She didn't like me, that's all there was to it.

Pause.

HE: Go on.

SHE: That time, the time I was telling you about, it was eight o'clock. The moon was round and red, like a cheese.

HE: Red cheese?

SHE: Cheese made of blood. It was in the window. Watching… warm.

HE: Warm? What was? Reverend Mother, one of the sisters, you? You didn't tell me that.

SHE: The moon. The moon was warm… Anyway, it felt warm. Reverend Mother was watching us. I felt scared. I could hear footsteps in the corridor. There was a bell somewhere…like an animal crying. All the sisters, just sitting there in silence, lifting their spoons up and down. Staring into space, chewing. Eating their cold soup.

HE: Cold, like your feet are?

SHE: How do you know?

HE: Because they are. Go on.

Pause.

SHE: I was trying so hard. My cheeks were all puffed out. I hate cornflour. It was slimy.

HE: How was it slimy? Like what? Tell me. Slimy like what?

SHE: I don't know. Like a guava, like a newborn baby, like a wet rat.

HE: Wet, like you?

SHE: How do you…?

HE: Good. Very good. Go on.

Pause.

SHE: I was always telling them I didn't like soup, that it was disgusting, especially cornflour soup, because it reminded me of my mother.

HE: That's not uncommon. My mother wasn't so much disgusting as pitiful. Go on.

SHE: It was disgusting because it reminded me of the soup my mother used to make - cold watery soup. It was the soup that was disgusting. Not my mother. I feel pity for her sometimes, but not disgust. It's different.

HE: What else?

SHE: Well, they took no notice. Every time I complained, they made me say the 'Our Father' over and over again. 'None of your whingeing,' that's what they used to say. They'd make me kneel down on thistles and recite 'Our Fathers'… over and over again. Under the altar. The huge big empty altar. With its candles…smelling of grease, of rancid fat. The sisters stood over me. If I got the words wrong, I had to start all over again. It worked. I felt…punished. That time, that time in particular, they didn't care that the soup was making me feel sick. I asked if I could go to the toilet.

HE: You needed to defecate?

SHE: No. I just needed to go to the toilet. To get out of there… to let things settle. I must have insisted too much because Reverend Mother got cross and started shouting. She wouldn't let me go.

HE: What was she shouting?

SHE: I don't remember. Terrible things…they scared me. She tried to make me swallow. She took the spoon and filled it with soup. Up to my mouth and down to the bowl, again and again, into my mouth and back down to the bowl.

HE: How many times?

SHE: I didn't count. A lot. The sisters were staring. They weren't scared, but they were staring. My teeth hurt. I thought I was going to be sick. I could feel my eyes filling up. I wasn't crying. But the tears were streaming from my eyes. I could see the moon in the window, like a big stain in the middle of the window, filling up like I was filling up.

It filled with water and I filled with soup. Me with soup and the moon with water.

Pause.

HE: What happened then?

SHE: I said something. No, I don't remember. No, I did say something. Reverend Mother got cross, then everything suddenly went dark and quiet… Then I remember her with her fists full of hair…my hair. It'd come away in her hand when she'd banged my head onto the table. A big hard wooden table.

HE: Was she very angry?

SHE: She was dirty, but she was angry too. Mostly dirty. I couldn't help it.

HE: What? What could you not help?

SHE: It's embarrassing.

HE: Tell me.

SHE: It's embarrassing.

HE: Tell me.

Pause.

SHE: The sick.

HE: Who was sick?

SHE: She was.

HE: Why?

SHE: Because it was disgusting.

HE: What was?

SHE: My face.

HE: Your face? Why?

SHE: Because it was covered in sick.

HE: She splashed you with sick?

SHE: Yes, but not really. I started it. The soup stuck in my throat, and I threw it up all over her habit. She held back for as long as she could, she was very particular, and she didn't vomit very much. That's what they told me. She blessed herself before she did. It splashed all over me, over my face and hair. The sisters were giggling. The rest isn't funny. Not that that bit was, but the rest was even less funny.

HE: What is the rest?

SHE: She did what she'd threatened to do. Please let me turn on the light.

HE: No, it's getting late. It's cold. It'll be time to go to sleep soon. There's no need to turn anything on. So what happened in the end?

SHE: I had to wash down the floors in the middle of the night. The bit before the end was what she threatened. She threatened that if I didn't swallow the soup, if I spat it out, like I did sometimes, she told me…she told me that… And that's what she did.

HE: Did what?

SHE: That.

HE: What 'that'?

SHE: That. She spooned it into me.

HE: And you let her?

Pause.

SHE: How could I stop her?

HE: You let her.

SHE: She said that what God has blessed may not be wantonly wasted. That it was for my own good. I had to learn. That's what it was about. Learning to please the Lord.

HE: Unbelievable.

SHE: She said you shouldn't take the Lord's name in vain. She said that was why she was carrying out her threat. If she hadn't have done that, she'd have had to do something far worse.

HE: She's right. God's a stunted little bully. He loves humiliating…punishing. That's why he makes so many demands.

SHE: Yes, and I was scared. God's fury. And the Reverend Mother's. Together. It was too much for me.

HE: As if that means anything! They're just empty words.

SHE: I was scared. I felt ashamed.

HE: That other thing – the something far worse…would you have told me?

SHE: I'm not sure. The bit about me having to swallow her sick was enough. Anyway I can't imagine what far worse thing she could have thought up.

HE: Tell me again.

SHE: What?

HE: One more time, please. Tell me again.

SHE: It's not a good idea. It's late. I can come tomorrow. I'll tell you again tomorrow.

HE: All right. Tomorrow. Pass me my drink... No, closer. Closer.

SHE moves towards him and holds out his drink. HE coughs.

SHE: You shouldn't be drinking. You don't sound well. You'll make yourself worse.

HE: What could be worse? This nothing life...that's God's real fury.

SHE: You're scaring me.

HE: You've lovely legs, sturdy, strong legs. Smooth skin.

SHE: How would you know? Maybe.

HE: Maybe. Cover yourself. Make sure nobody sees you on the way out.

SHE: I will.

HE: Come back tomorrow and tell me if they've found him, what people are saying. I'd like to know. Come back tomorrow. I need to know.

SHE: I do too. I'd like to.

HE: Come back tomorrow. Early. Tomorrow.

SHE: I'll be here.

2

SHE is standing beside the door, which is now closed, waiting, holding a tray. HE is sitting on the bed. HE becomes progressively agitated.

HE: At first it's like you were being rocked. A slow sleepy rocking feeling. Then nausea. Burning, like fingernails scraping down the inside of your throat. Your arm...

SHE: Can I do anything? Your arm, you said, señor?

27

HE: Sssh. My arm, always the same one.

SHE: The same arm?

HE: My left arm, like some ridiculous, useless, limp…rag. You can't move it. You can't breathe, then you start sweating, your head's spinning with fever, and everything, all the normal things, change…

SHE: Your drink, señor?

HE: You don't understand any of this. You're still young. Come over here. It's like…you were moving through thick air, or floating uselessly inside some dense liquid, like spit. And you feel like a fool, like one of those fish with great big staring eyes that never see enough to stop themselves from being caught. The minutes stretch out in front of you, not moving, and time drags on endlessly. Things, objects, have a sort of echo, they spill out over their own edges. Your eyes are closed and there's no darkness, your head feels hollow, like it's been scooped out, but it's not quiet inside. You look out from a place that's already deep inside your eyes. Sounds are muffled, they lose their clarity, they slow down. Everything that's happening, it's happening inside you, that's how it feels. You feel an inertia that permeates everything, that disorientates you. Then you get the feeling…

Pause.

You don't know what I'm talking about, do you? Do you want to know?

SHE: No. Go on.

HE: The feeling of things blurring, of terrible pressure. And then a surge of unstoppable anxiety. That's what I'm talking about. The walls close in around you, they threaten you, the light mists over. Everything becomes…like an enemy. Grotesque and deformed. And you're able to watch

28

– I mean you can actually watch – how one of your eyes, usually it's your left eye, or it's always your left eye, and the whole left side of your head, they swell up and separate and are about to explode. And before that happens, they burst inside your head, in the most horrible detail: you see your arteries swirling with blood clots that could block them at any moment…you can feel the flow getting weaker, the flow of your polluted blood…

SHE: Señor…

HE: Your pulse pounding in your forehead, your teeth clenched, the paralysing pain, again and again and again…and that terrible desire to bite, to bite and beat and to break whatever it is so that you can drag it down with you, so you don't have to go on your own. Life's final useless gesture, to destroy. To keep your terror at bay, to inhabit the silence, to sink your nails into that one last moment, not to allow the light and that last flickering voice of consciousness to fade, to die. That final terror of going on your own… Because you disappear and…then there's nothing.

Pause. The rain can be seen through the window.

Look. It's still falling. It won't stop. Did you notice?

SHE: Do you mind if I go now?

HE: Answer me. I asked you a question, I believe.

SHE: Sorry…what was it?

HE: Whether you noticed. It hasn't stopped. Like yesterday.

SHE: Yes. It doesn't seem to have. And it won't.

HE: It won't stop. What sense is there to it? Can you tell me? Is there any?

SHE: Sorry?

HE: The rain, snow, the way trees slowly defy the law of gravity. Is there any purpose to it?

SHE: I suppose there must be.

HE: You suppose, eh. You suppose. What is it you suppose?

SHE: I don't know. There's some reason. Everything's here for a reason.

HE: What reason? Nothing changes anything. If we weren't here, things like that would just go on the same, regardless. They were here before us and there was no sense to them. Whatever sense they have now, it was us that gave it to them. We invented it because we wanted to. And we invented time. How else would we measure our failure, our decay? A yardstick for our crumbling bodies. What else are we – bags filled with flesh and fluids, that's all. And the bags get old, they rot, and they burst.

SHE: I don't understand. I don't know.

HE: So you don't understand, and you don't know and you don't worry about eternity, and why things are here for no reason. The simple things.

SHE: Simple things?

HE: Like this endless rain. Do you think it cares whether you and I are cold or frightened or don't understand? And do you know the worst thing, it's that all our will-power is focussed on not wanting to lose it, on wishing our life would go on for ever, on wanting to explain the senselessness of it. Because we're ruled by desire, animals driven by desire.

Pause.

You can close the window now.

SHE: I should be going.

HE: You haven't done what I asked.

SHE gives him the drink and goes to close the window. HE follows her with his eyes, caressing her with his gaze.

You're very young. Do you dye your hair?

SHE: What? No.

HE: So that's your real colour. Good. That would be senseless. Although if nothing has any sense, then why not? But that's your natural colour, you say. You can never account for beauty. If it's there at all, it's in spite of ourselves. There's no need to be embarrassed. What's your name?

SHE: Sorry, I'm not allowed…

HE: You're not allowed? To have a name? What stupid rule prevents you from having a name? Tell me your name.

SHE: Sorry.

HE: Then tell me this: do you still believe in God?

SHE: I can't…

HE: You can't believe?

SHE: I'm not…

HE: So what can you do? Just stand there fiddling with the hem of your skirt? You're nervous.

SHE: Your hands.

HE: What about them?

SHE: They're…very elegant.

HE: Thank you.

SHE: They're…

HE: What? What are they?

SHE: Nothing… I was just imagining… It's late.

HE: Have you been working here long?

SHE: No.

HE: Are you new?

SHE: No.

HE: Then?

SHE: I'm not allowed. To talk, I mean…

HE: Not allowed? Why not? What they pay you for making beds, is it enough to buy that too? Does their money buy every single hour of your day? Everything your hands do? Now that sounds tempting, sinful even. The silences you're so keen to keep? Everything you do with your mouth? Every word you speak, few and far between though your words are? All of that for a few notes and a handful of coins a week? That's what they bought from you when you started work here? And your name into the bargain? I could pay more.

SHE: Good night.

HE: No, don't go. Please. I didn't intend to cause any offence. Well, I don't think I did. I wasn't suggesting anything, and I wouldn't…unless you wanted me to. There's no need to be…worried. This would be beneficial to both of us. I would be free to ask you for whatever, and you would feel freed, released, from the oppressive conditions of your employment. So, a little space of freedoms…for us both. What do you think? We could share my drink.

SHE: It's not allowed. I have to go.

HE: You're shivering.

SHE: I'm cold.

HE: I think it's warm.

SHE: But I'm cold.

HE: I'd like us to talk.

SHE: Some other time. Good night.

HE: Good morning. It's past midnight.

SHE: Good morning, then.

HE: You're beautiful and warm…like fruit ripening.

SHE: I don't know what you're talking about.

HE: Stay a moment. Just one moment.

SHE: I have to go.

HE: Please. You can go in a minute. I just want to look at you. Stay still.

Pause. HE circles her, close enough to catch her scent. HE looks at her from behind.

SHE: You're scaring me.

HE: Don't turn round. Wait, please. Please. There's no rush. I wouldn't do the slightest thing to make you…anxious. Take a look at me and you'll see for yourself. There's nothing to be scared of. I'm not asking you to have a drink to take advantage of you; I don't mind one way or another, but it'll stop you shivering. I don't want to be alone. All I'm asking you to do is listen. And talk.

SHE: Talk? I don't know how to talk.

HE: That's a lie. You may not like talking, but you can't not talk. You have to talk to say you don't know how to talk. And that makes you an object of…considerable fascination. Take care, because sooner or later it'll cause you problems. Or pleasure. Naïvety is perverse.

SHE: I'm not.

HE: Naïve or perverse?

SHE: Neither.

HE: Another lie.

SHE: I have to go.

HE: I suppose you do. I'm going to be here for some time. Are you in every day?

SHE: I live here.

HE: All the better. I'm enjoying this drink. Will you bring me another one tomorrow?

SHE: You can order it from whoever's on tomorrow.

HE: You're on now and I'm ordering one for tomorrow.

SHE: Somebody else might bring it up.

HE: I'll ask for you; we'll say you made a good impression, and I was generous. I gave you a good tip.

SHE: There's no need.

HE: Here. Take it.

SHE: If you like.

SHE goes to take it. HE catches her hand. SHE pulls it away immediately.

HE: Do *you* like? That's what makes sense, makes sense of things. Me telling you to do it, which I'm not by the way, that isn't enough. I don't need some sort of object in a skirt. I want you to want to bring me the drink, to like bringing me the drink. It's wanting that makes sense; desire gives pleasure, and only pleasure makes sense, no matter what it costs.

SHE: I can bring your drink.

HE: Do you want to?

SHE: I don't know.

HE: You can't not know. I want – I need – you to.

SHE: Ninet brought it up yesterday.

HE: Now I know her name. I'm not interested in her bringing it though. I'm interested in you doing it.

SHE: Me? Why me?

HE: Because you listen.

SHE: I don't know.

HE: You've said that.

SHE: That's because I don't know. I'll think about it.

HE: No need to knock. The door'll be open.

3

They are sitting opposite each other.

SHE: There was a man. Watching.

HE: Watching? How did that make you feel?

SHE: Hot.

HE: Because he was watching you?

SHE: Perhaps.

HE: Where was he watching from?

SHE: There was a crack in the wall.

HE: How do you know it was a man?

SHE: By the way he was looking. It was a man's look. Like dogs look, when they're in heat.

HE: And you saw him?

SHE: Or I dreamt it. I could see his eye, his great green wet eye watching us. We were trying not to make any noise. My mother was suspicious.

HE: Who was it?

SHE: I don't know.

HE: What was she suspicious of?

SHE: What we'd been playing. I must have been about eleven.

HE: Very good. You didn't waste any time.

SHE: He was my cousin.

HE: Who was watching you or who was playing with you?

SHE: Playing. My cousin. I don't know who the man was. We were playing.

HE: Playing? At what?

SHE: The way everyone does. Doctors. First, he was a doctor. Then he was a holy man.

HE: A holy man? Interesting choice. Are you going to tell me?

SHE: I will. If you want.

HE: I do.

SHE moves closer.

SHE: I had this awful disease. My body was covered in spots.

HE: What sort of spots?

SHE: Red and black ones. And leisures. Is that what they're called?

HE: What do you mean?

SHE: When like a line opens up on your skin and blood comes out, you can get it on your back or on the bottom of your foot.

HE: Lesions.

SHE: That's right. Lesions. He said he was a miracle doctor, that he could cure my spots and les...lesions.

HE: And did he?

SHE: I think so. He took off my blouse. He said I had two on my chest, which was very serious.

HE: Two lesions.

SHE: Two spots. And they weren't red or black. They were pink. He told me he wasn't surprised and that they seemed to be getting worse because they were getting puffy. In a year's time the puffiness would be very noticeable and I'd have problems.

HE: What sort of problems?

SHE: Everyone'd be looking at them and they'd know what I had under my blouse and I'd have to use crutches, or something like that.

HE: You mean a stick?

SHE: A bra, he said.

HE: And you didn't know what that was?

SHE: No.

HE: How many years ago was this?

SHE: A few now. Not that many.

HE: And how old was your cousin?

SHE: Six years older than me.

HE: Ah... Tell me more.

SHE: Well, he told me they were getting puffy because they were full of poison, that he would use an old Indian trick, that he would suck them to get the badness out, and that would cure me.

HE: And what did he do?

SHE: He sucked them.

HE: Where exactly did you have the spots?

SHE: I can't say.

HE: You can't say?

SHE: No.

HE: You can't or you won't?

SHE: I can't. It's too embarrassing.

HE: Did he cure you?

SHE: At first, yes, I thought he had. But after a few months the little spots were still getting bigger and it scared me. I told my mother I was very sick. I said the spots had grown. She asked me what did I mean, spots. And I told her everything. She asked me all sorts of questions. She made me take my clothes off, in the sitting room, in front of the gentleman.

HE: What gentleman, the one who'd been watching you?

SHE: No. Her new friend. She said he was my uncle. I had a new uncle every week.

HE: So what happened?

SHE: My uncle, that uncle, he tried as well one day, he tried to get the poison out. My mother found out. She wasn't pleased. To get me out of the way, she sent me to the nuns.

HE: Why?

SHE: Because of the spots and the lesions.

HE: What lesions? You didn't have any lesions.

SHE: I did. One. Between my legs.

HE: I see. And did your cousin cure that as well?

SHE: I think so. But in a different way. The first few times though he sucked too.

HE: And what did you feel?

SHE: Like itchy, tickly. I felt embarrassed.

HE: Did it hurt?

SHE: Not when he was sucking. It was tickly. First it was my spots, then my lesion. One time…

Pause.

HE: Tell me.

SHE: Can I come a bit closer?

HE: If you like.

SHE: Is it okay like this?

HE: That's very close.

SHE: It's okay like this. Well, one time, when he was curing my lesion, something went right through me.

HE: Really?

SHE: Yes. It made me feel strange, as if I'd been shaken by a flame, an electrical flame.

39

HE: A current.

SHE: No, a flame.

HE: All right, a flame. What else?

SHE: He got cross. He stopped curing me after that.

HE: He left your lesion alone.

SHE: More or less. Until he thought up the thing about the devil and hell.

HE: The devil and hell, what was that?

SHE: Nothing. A dirty story just.

HE: Tell me it.

SHE: I can't remember.

HE: Tell me anyway, whatever you can remember.

SHE: There's no point.

HE: Did he make the story up?

SHE: He heard it in school. Somebody told him it in Logic, that's what he said.

HE: Well?

SHE: Well, there was this very holy girl who wanted to serve God. And someone said to her that in a village nearby, or fairly nearby, there was a holy man who knew all the best ways to serve God. He was very poor, and a very holy man, and he lived in the desert.

HE: So he lived in a village, but in the desert as well?

SHE: Yes. The thing was that the girl wanted to meet him. She told her parents and went off to the forest to find him.

HE: I thought he lived in the desert.

40

SHE: He did. But she had to go through the forest to get to the desert. The story has to be logical, doesn't it? And she got lost on the way. The girl got lost. And somebody sent her the wrong way a couple of times, but eventually she found him. Very thin, with a big long beard. And all he ever had to eat were green apples and roots and water. That's what he offered the girl when she arrived. Oh, and a vine leaf.

HE: A vine leaf? What for?

SHE: So that she knew what they looked like. The holy man said she had to gather piles of them to make her bed, because he didn't have another bed and he didn't want her to have to sleep on the floor and because he was holy, and a man and not a fool, he wasn't going to catch his death of cold sleeping there himself. So the girl had to hurry up because it was almost night-time…

HE: Vine leaves in the desert.

SHE: It was a test of faith.

HE: And what has all that, the bed made out of vine leaves and faith, what has all that got to do with the story about the devil and hell and your lesion that couldn't be cured?

SHE: Wait. Well, one day, after a lot of fasting, and watching the girl kneeling in the river washing his socks, the holy man had an illumination. He told her he'd been possessed by a devil that wouldn't leave him in peace, and that God, all-seeing and good as he is, had led her there providentially to help him and to serve him. And so he explained to her where her hell was and where his devil was and for a week they set about trying to lock the devil back up. But then the girl started to really like dousing the burning flames of hell and she wanted to lock the devil up as often as possible, but the holy man, who wasn't as young as he used to be, soon got fed up with it and he sent her home, and her parents married her off to someone else.

HE: I see. He used that story to cajole you, and he cured you with his devil… Until he got fed up.

SHE: He didn't have time to get fed up. That's when my mother found out what was going on with the…

HE: The spots.

SHE: That's right. The spots.

HE: So go on then.

SHE: And she packed me off to the nuns.

Pause.

HE: You haven't finished. You didn't tell me what happened to the bed made out of vine leaves.

SHE: I don't know that bit.

He coughs.

SHE: Are you okay?

HE: Yes. It's nothing.

SHE: Are you sure? It's a bad cough.

HE: I'm okay.

SHE: Shall we go on?

HE: No. I'm fed up now. You can go.

SHE: It's still early.

HE: I'm tired. Go on. Close the door behind you.

4

They are both standing. After a silence, SHE goes to take away the glass which he has just drained. SHE puts it on the tray and walks to the door. HE closes it.

HE: I have a request. Something very simple…very easy.

SHE: Yes.

HE: No questions.

SHE: What is it?

HE: You didn't listen.

SHE: I heard you.

HE: You and I share something. These dark times.

SHE: Bad times?

HE: No.

SHE: Then why dark?

HE: Because it's night-time. Times, at night.

SHE: I'm doing my job, that's all. Doing what I'm paid to do.

HE: And I'm barely surviving.

SHE: Do you really feel so sick?

HE: No. No sicker than usual.

SHE: It's usual to feel sick?

HE: It becomes usual. The important thing is not to waste your time weeping. Only cowards weep.

SHE: I don't cry ever. And it's not that I've never been hurt.

HE: Being with me, does that…hurt you? Has it?

SHE: No.

HE: Good.

SHE: Is it going to?

HE: No, of course it won't. Not much anyway. Would it matter?

SHE: I don't know.

HE: Would you do things? Things, if I asked you to?

SHE: I don't know.

HE: I could pay.

SHE: There's no need. A normal tip's enough.

HE: I insist.

SHE: No. Don't. The others would suspect.

HE: Have they said anything?

SHE: No.

HE: Have they asked you anything?

SHE: No.

HE: What if they did?

SHE: I'd tell them.

HE: What would you tell them?

SHE: That there's nothing going on.

HE: That's the truth.

SHE: All I do is bring you up your drink.

HE: That's all.

SHE: Anything else is because I choose to.

HE: That's the dangerous bit, the bit that matters. The anything else. And the way you say it.

SHE: Why?

HE: Because saying it like that makes it sound…suspicious. They might be suspicious about us, say things about us…

SHE: Suspicious? Do you think so?

HE: Yes, I do.

SHE: But nobody does ask me.

HE: Do they not?

SHE: No. They're usually asleep by this time.

HE: They know you've been here?

SHE: But they don't know how long I stayed. I'm always the last one in bed.

HE: That's good.

SHE: What was your request?

HE: Nothing important.

SHE: Tell me.

HE: Nothing. It's nothing.

SHE: You're very annoying.

HE: Why? Am I hurting you?

SHE: No, but now I want to know.

HE: I want to know too.

SHE: Want to know what?

HE: Time enough for that. But we have to get one thing clear from the start: this is our secret. We have to maintain our...intimacy.

SHE: You use big words.

HE: Big words?

SHE: Like...'intimacy'.

HE: Big?

SHE: No but...it makes me feel important. Like...maybe... some time...

HE: This is some time. Our time. And yes, you are important. Very important. To me.

SHE: Don't say things like that.

HE: You don't like...things like that?

SHE: I get embarrassed.

HE: There's no reason to.

SHE: They make me go red.

HE: You blush.

SHE: All right, I blush.

HE: Your eyes...

SHE: What about my eyes?

HE: They're...subtly malevolent. Light, childlike, malevolent.

SHE: They're not light.

HE: They shine.

SHE: Like a light?

HE: They electrify.

SHE: What?

HE: It doesn't matter.

SHE: I have a right to know.

HE: Yes, you do have a right. So listen. Creatures like you usually bring ruin to themselves, and to the unwary, like me.

SHE: Unwary? Like you?

HE: Like me.

SHE: I don't want to do you any harm.

HE: No. Nobody ever wants to. But one day you'll understand that love is never more sensuous than when it's doing harm. We can't avoid hurting other people. That's what desire is.

SHE: You know things.

HE: No more than you do. No more than you. You know everything you need to.

SHE: What do I know?

HE: How important you are to me. That's twice I've said it. Your advantage. The coin's in the air.

SHE: Are we...playing some sort of game?

HE: That's exactly what we're doing.

SHE: What are the rules?

HE: No rules.

SHE: What do I have to do to win?

HE: Nothing. Absolutely nothing.

SHE: So...?

HE: Just be beautiful.

47

SHE: Me?

HE: Simply that.

SHE: And am I?

HE: You've no idea how much you are. Or how you are.

Pause.

SHE: That's all I have to do?

HE: That's all. That's how to win. How you've won already.

SHE: So what is the game?

HE: It's about not letting yourself be dragged down.

SHE: I don't understand.

HE: What you love the most can hurt you the most. You have to get what you want, and you might get hurt, but you have to keep yourself intact.

SHE: That's the game?

HE: Yes, it is. Do you understand?

SHE: So we have to love each other?

HE: That's right. But keeping ourselves intact at the same time. We balance on the ledge. Frightening, isn't it?

SHE: No. I want to play. When do we start?

5

HE is standing, anxiously. SHE is sitting in a chair, reading.

SHE: I want to ask you something. Can I?

HE: Not now.

SHE: It's important.

HE: Later. Finish this first.

SHE: What does 'feral' mean?

HE: What else does it say?

SHE: But I want to know what it means. Feral. Is it something bad?

HE: No. Keep reading.

SHE: How am I going to understand if you won't tell me what feral means? Is it an insult?

HE: No. It's not an insult.

SHE: Okay. It's just that it says that the man, when he was detained…

HE: He was helping with enquiries.

SHE: No, it says 'detained'.

HE: Bloody fools, journalists.

SHE: 'When he was detained, he accused the woman of being an abject liar, vile, and feral.' That's why I thought it was an insult. I understand all the rest of it, apart from 'abject', so I thought 'feral' and 'abject' were insults too.

HE: No. It's just a way of saying 'wild'. It's not an insult, though it may sound like one here. Feral. You talk about cats being feral. Fools the lot of them.

SHE: Where do they find words like that?

HE: From their dictionaries. Their dictionaries make up for their lack of imagination, they expand their narrow horizons. What have cats got to do with this? What else does it say?

SHE: A whole lot. Do you want me to read it or just tell you?

HE: I'd prefer you read it.

SHE: It says: 'Suicide Plunge Chambermaid: Body still not Found.'

HE: Very eloquent.

SHE: 'The chambermaid, who worked in a well-known city-centre hotel, had alleged that a guest, a teacher of languages...'

HE: Journalists...useless every last one of them.

SHE: '...a teacher of languages had made improper sexual advances when, around midnight, he summoned her to bring a triple brandy to his room. The teacher vehemently denied her allegations, but was detained and taken to the police station where he in turn accused the woman of being an abject liar, vile and feral.'

HE: So it says he was the one who said 'feral'.

SHE: It looks like it.

HE: Well, they're wrong. If he is a teacher, even if he were a language teacher, assuming that the hacks haven't got that wrong as well, he would know what 'feral' means. Any bloody queer hairdresser would know what 'feral' means.

SHE: Will I go on?

HE: Yes.

SHE: 'The teacher, who is a worker in...'

HE: Who's a worker! What does that mean? That he makes cars? Worker...

SHE: '...a worker in a prestigious foreign university, he had come here on holiday after having undertaken the translation of a book of philosophy...'

HE: This is unbelievable. He may be a philologist, or a mathematician or a philosopher, but not a 'teacher of languages'. No half-baked teacher of languages can actually manage to string more than a few words together in any language other than their own. Sometimes not even that. Never mind translate a book of philosophy.

SHE: '…and was recovering from a severe bout of flu. He had been confined to bed for several days as a result of the sudden change of climate.'

HE: 'Confined to bed'. Wonderful. So as well as a teacher of languages he's some sort of maniac.

SHE: 'When it was concluded that the teacher of languages was in no fit state to seduce the chambermaid, let alone commit any act of sexual aggression, he was released after several hours and returned to the said hotel. But later he checked out.'

Pause.

HE: Is that it?

SHE: No. There's more.

HE: Finish it.

SHE: 'The chambermaid was sacked and when she saw a photograph of herself in the paper under the headline "Tarred with her own brush", she threw herself into the river. To date, no body has been found.'

HE: Anything else?

SHE: No.

HE: Nothing about the teacher?

SHE: No. Other than what I read.

HE: No photo?

SHE: No.

HE: People, what are they saying?

SHE: Not a thing.

HE: What do you mean, not a thing?

SHE: Just that. Not a thing. It's the sort of thing that happens every day.

HE: People always have something to say, even about things that happen every day. It keeps the boredom at bay. It gives them something to think about.

SHE: I don't know. I think she's not the only one.

HE: What do you mean?

SHE: What I said: I think she's not the only one. Or the first one to throw herself into the river.

HE: Where did you get that idea from?

SHE: Nowhere. Just a guess.

Pause.

I want to ask you something.

HE: I've already answered.

SHE: Don't get cross.

HE: I'm not getting cross. It's not you. It's me. I'm glad you're here.

SHE: So, can I?

HE: 'Feral' isn't an insult.

SHE: It's not about that.

HE: About what then?

SHE: I don't know if I should.

HE: I don't know if I can.

Pause. HE stops behind her and slips his hand onto her neck. Startled, SHE stands up.

SHE: I don't need to any more.

HE: Why not? What's wrong?

SHE: There's light…some light outside the window.

HE: What of it?

SHE: I should go and a look. There might be somebody there, watching.

HE: There's no one watching. Don't worry. Stay.

SHE: No. I'm going to look.

HE: I haven't answered you.

SHE: I haven't asked you.

HE: So you don't want to know?

SHE: I'm not sure. The way you look at me, it…

HE: It what?

SHE: It scares me.

Pause.

HE: So you don't want me to tell you?

SHE: Tell me what?

HE: Whatever it is you want to know.

SHE: Are you shivering?

HE: I'm cold.

SHE: But it's warm…don't you think? I'm going to see who's out there. Maybe someone's looking for me.

She leaves.

HE: All I meant was…

6

They are both sitting on the bed, looking at photographs, perhaps on a laptop.

SHE: What else?

HE: It's the idea behind it. It's always the same idea. Look at this one.

SHE: It's disgusting.

HE: No, it's not. Look more closely.

SHE: It's the same as the other one.

HE: No. It's not. It might look the same. But it's not.

SHE: I don't know what you mean.

HE: It's not just what's in the picture. It's the idea. I don't know where it comes from. And I don't know how I came to believe it. But it's there. Right from your childhood you hear things and you see things that insinuate it, the idea. All sorts of things, stupid things, trivial things, to do with men and women.

SHE: Men and women?

HE: Yes. It's in everything, all around you. In pictures. In words. In the way people talk to each other. What they say. And you end up believing it, the lie. You've no choice. The first time I did it, it hurt me more than her.

SHE: How?

HE: I don't know. Maybe it wasn't the right time.

SHE: Why not?

HE: I was too young. I wasn't ready.

SHE: Ready for what?

HE: The idea, to believe it. All the time you're growing up, people warn you, they try to get you ready, they tell you all the time. They're training you. To hurt. To cause pain. And I tried. I really did. But even though I didn't want to, in the end I'd no choice but to believe it. Look at this one.

SHE: Maybe it is hurting, but they're enjoying it.

HE: Look. We're all different, but the idea's the same, and it works the same way in all of us. It's life, it's a vision of the world.

SHE: They are enjoying it.

HE: Who are?

SHE: Them. The women. Look at them.

HE: Well so they should. They're stronger. They're made for it, they're built for pain.

SHE: No. We're not.

HE: Well, of course, they like it in some sort of way.

SHE: But there's more to it than just pain.

HE: Well, why else would they do it? It's the pain they enjoy. That's the idea.

SHE: Money. That's why they do it.

HE: Just money? No. Look at them. They're hardly wasting away.

SHE: Neither are the men. Look at the muscles on them.

HE: But they hardly ever show their faces…you know why, don't you?

SHE: No…I've never seen stuff like this before.

HE: Honestly?

SHE: Honestly.

HE: Not even at school?

SHE: No.

HE: So what do you think?

SHE: It's strange. It makes me feel strange. I like it, but…I don't know, it repels me too.

HE: It's all about the same idea, everything has to do with that. When that feeling of aggression is thwarted or frustrated, so that instead of feeling pain the woman seems to share the pleasure, the man reacts, he rears up like a…wild animal. Because that's what the idea is – it's about tearing apart, bursting, ripping, pushing inside as hard and deep as you can, splitting her, pulling her apart, until you break her. Look at this one.

SHE: Wow! That's unbelievable. How's that possible?

HE: Very easy. Pure strength…and experience. He's…

SHE: I meant her, not him. That's just the way he's built. He was born like that. But she…

HE: I wouldn't be so sure. It's a trick shot, maybe an implant. They use all sorts of creams and potions and injections.

SHE: It looks real.

HE: It looks.

SHE: But she's…enormous, incredible. She's taken all of it. She's full. Run right through. So smoothly.

HE: No. That's not how it works. It's the other way round. He's dominating her, but she likes it.

SHE: I don't know.

HE: What's it like for you?

SHE: Well.

HE: Tell me.

SHE: My idea is different. It's how long it goes on for.

HE: How long it goes on?

SHE: Yes, until you're exhausted.

HE: Until it hurts?

SHE: Maybe.

HE: Until you feel you could die?

SHE: Maybe.

HE: Why not? Until you die… But men, we…

SHE: You?

HE: The whole experience is different for us. Look.

SHE: Why different?

HE: The feeling of invading, stretching, flooding. It's powerful. A very powerful feeling. Domination. We have different tools. The privilege of being a man.

SHE: Well perhaps… But domination…

HE: Why 'perhaps'?

SHE: Is that what you really think?

HE: Yes. Look at this one.

SHE: No. Look at this one.

HE: What?

SHE: Look at it. He's weak...he looks puny. And she's strong, I
mean really strong. She's bored.

HE: She's a barrel.

SHE: No, she's beautiful. Strong.

HE: He looks strong too.

SHE: Not like her. He can't manage. His tool...

HE: What about it?

SHE: It's small. Hers is bigger. She's devouring him,
swallowing him whole, wolfing him down. And she's got
room for more.

HE: You find that sometimes; there are women like bottomless
pits; like looking into an abyss. They're fat. They're nearly
always fat.

SHE: She's not.

HE: She's on the fat side.

SHE: I don't think she is. Look at this one.

HE: What about it?

SHE: She's with three of them. You couldn't imagine one of
them being with three of her.

HE: It happens.

SHE: Only in men's fantasies

HE: No, any of them could do it...look at the size of them.
Some of them have got huge ones.

SHE: You can imagine somebody like her with three big
men...but imagine three of her with just one of them, even
the biggest one.

HE: What?

SHE: He couldn't cope.

HE: He couldn't? Not even him?

SHE: No, he couldn't.

HE: Bah! It's just your opinion, that's all.

SHE: That's what you think?

HE: Of course it is. So now it's not her who's been run through, ripped, and burst, and instead she's wolfing him down, devouring him, dominating him?

SHE: It looks that way.

Pause.

HE: You're wrong.

SHE: Am I?

HE: Yes, you are. You're wrong. That's what I meant, what I was telling you about, when you're thwarted or frustrated, I mean as an aggressor, it builds up into a sort of crescendo and it drives you wild. Look at the photographs. Look at the men, there are more and more of them with her, taking her, doing it to her,

SHE: It doesn't sound too bad. Like in this one?

HE: I don't think you understand. Look – imagine three or four men like him, each with a thing like that, and two more waiting to have their turn with you, getting themselves worked up watching you, and imagine that you're like her…

SHE: The skinny one?

HE: Yes, like the skinny one. Imagine them, like rhinoceroses with their horns, goring you, each one of them again and again, for hours on end. Imagine them using you, emptying themselves into you, and they've left you broken...they've split you wide open and left you there, and you're half dead and they're resting before they begin all over again.

SHE: I've got to imagine that?

HE: Yes. Look...like that and like that and like that.

SHE: Uh huh.

HE: Imagine.

Pause.

SHE: Uh huh.

HE: Now do you think you've devoured them, you've wolfed them down, you've eaten them alive? Do you think you dominated them? Do you? Really?

SHE: Yes. In a way.

HE: No you don't. No way at all. That's plain stupidity. I don't know why you're so obstinate.

SHE: All I'm doing is looking at the pictures and imagining what you're telling me to. Señor.

HE: Why are you being so obstinate?

SHE: Do you not know the story?

HE: What story?

SHE: The one about the master and his slave.

HE: That's different. It's got nothing to do with this.

SHE: No, I suppose it doesn't. It's just that both of them create their own roles. The master and his slave. They swap roles.

HE: Exactly. You have to accept the role. And the story. These pictures all tell a story. One single story: that's why they were made, to show the splitting and the ripping and the invading, the supreme pleasure of violence, the supremacy of the aggressor, and that's why you need a tool like this.

SHE: Whose tool?

HE: A tool. Look forget it. That's enough.

SHE: I'm sleepy.

HE: Fine.

SHE: Is it?

HE: Yes, it is. People get sleepy at night.

SHE: It's not that late. I just feel like going to bed…

Pause.

Do you mind?

HE: No, I don't mind.

Pause.

Well?

SHE: I'm waiting for you to…

HE: Good night then.

SHE: Is that it?

HE: Yes, that's it.

SHE: Sorry, I thought…

HE: You thought what?

SHE: Just…that's all you're going to say?

HE: Yes.

SHE: You don't want me to tell you things?

HE: No.

SHE: You don't want to know if I'm...

HE: No. I'm sure you are.

SHE: All right. It's okay. Good night. Tomorrow...

HE: Yes. Tomorrow, tomorrow, tomorrow.

SHE: Tomorrow.

7

In the doorway, one each side, leaning against the wall.

SHE: What do you think of me?

HE: Does it matter?

SHE: It does to me. A lot.

HE: What do you want to know?

SHE: The truth.

HE: The truth. Which one?

SHE: How do I seem to you?

HE: What is it you're asking?

SHE: Do you love me?

Pause.

HE: I'm not going to answer that.

SHE: People are saying.

HE: What do you mean?

SHE: That they're saying.

HE: What are they saying?

SHE: Nothing.

HE: Don't play with me.

SHE: I'm not. We're both playing.

HE: Tell me what people are saying.

SHE: Well, people, that's a very general thing.

HE: Abstract.

SHE: That's right, abstract.

HE: You mean, some people are saying?

SHE: Yes, maybe that's it. Some people are saying.

HE: And?

SHE: Others are listening.

HE: Just what are you driving at with this stupid rumour business?

SHE: I said 'saying'. 'Saying'.

HE: Gossiping.

SHE: 'Saying' sounds better.

HE: It's not the same thing.

SHE: There's not that much difference.

HE: All right. I haven't got the energy for this.

SHE: All right. I'll tell you.

HE: Good.

SHE: A couple of men were following me. In the street, one evening. I went for a walk because I had nothing else to do. Are you listening?

HE: Yes.

SHE: And watching?

HE: No.

> *HE stifles a cough.*

SHE: What are you doing?

HE: Nothing. Go on.

SHE: Are you sure?

HE: Yes.

SHE: They were calling after me…they came right up.

HE: Why were they following you?

SHE: I don't know.

HE: Did you do anything to encourage them?

SHE: Nothing. I was just walking.

HE: You were walking.

SHE: Yes, one evening, because I had nothing else to do. They whispered things at me.

HE: What things?

SHE: Things.

HE: What did you do?

SHE: Nothing. I listened. Men's things.

HE: What do you know about men's things?

SHE: Not very much, but I supposed they were men's things.

HE: What men's things did they say to you?

SHE: Can you not imagine?

HE: No.

SHE: If you saw me in the street, what things would you say?

HE: Nothing.

SHE: Nothing. Nothing at all?

HE: If I saw you in the street, parading like that, I'd think you were an idiot, but I wouldn't say anything. Not a word.

SHE: They said about my legs.

HE: Your legs?

SHE: They wanted to touch them.

HE: Did they?

SHE: No.

HE: What did they have to say about your legs?

SHE: That I'd lovely legs.

HE: Well, well.

SHE: They said about my breasts as well.

HE: Did they say you have spots, full of poison, and they'd have to suck them for you, like your cousin or your uncles?

SHE: Just one uncle. No, not exactly. They said about my backside too.

HE: And that's what people are gossiping about?

SHE: What they're saying. No. That's what the men were gossiping about. I wanted to know what you thought.

HE: I don't think anything. I don't care whether they say things or say nothing. It's your lookout.

SHE: The rain's cleared up. Nothing strange about going out for a walk. It's not as cold.

HE: No, it's not. I had noticed.

SHE: It's getting sunnier.

HE: Surprise, surprise.

SHE: It's getting warmer at night.

HE: Really. It's certainly getting harder to sleep. To breathe.

SHE: I'm wearing less clothes. Have you noticed? Have you?

HE: Even if I hadn't wanted to.

SHE: Do you know why?

HE: Because you're mad.

SHE: About…anyone?

HE: You're not. Don't even say it.

SHE: I put perfume on.

HE: I noticed that too.

SHE: You never say anything. But they said…

HE: That makes it less interesting.

SHE: Is that what you think?

HE: Absolutely.

SHE: All right.

> *SHE makes to go, but HE stops her brusquely.*

Hey. You're hurting me. Let go.

HE: What's happened to you?

SHE: Nothing.

HE: You've changed.

SHE: So have you. You seem cross all the time.

HE: Just tired. Frightened.

SHE: Do you feel sick?

HE: I said tired.

SHE: And frightened?

HE: It's nothing. It doesn't matter.

SHE: Did you not sleep well?

HE: That's not why I'm tired.

SHE: Then what's wrong?

HE: Is it not obvious?

SHE: No, it's not.

HE: Use your eyes.

SHE: How? With no light…

HE: All right!

SHE: Yes. I can see you and I can guess.

HE: Well then?

SHE: Well then what?

HE: You can't tell anything?

SHE: Not from your face.

HE: Can you hear my voice?

SHE: Yes.

HE: And what does it tell you?

SHE: What do you want it to tell me?

HE: How does it sound?

SHE: Hmm…well…

　　Pause.

HE: I'm done…finished.

SHE: Done?

HE: Old.

SHE: No. You're not so old.

HE: No?

SHE: No.

HE: What would you call it?

SHE: Call what?

HE: This. Look at me.

SHE: I don't know. You're the teacher.

HE: What did you say?

Pause.

SHE: That it's you who's teaching me.

HE: No. You didn't say it's me who's teaching you.

SHE: I said…

HE: Don't say it again. Don't even think about saying it outside these four walls.

SHE: It's the first time.

HE: Get out of here.

SHE: Don't talk to me like that.

HE: Get out of here. Now. I'm fed up.

SHE: It's not my fault.

HE: No, it's not, but I want to be on my own. I'm tired.

SHE: Before…

HE: Before. Before. Before. Things are different now.

SHE: Why are they different?

HE: You went out.

SHE: What's wrong with that?

HE: What's wrong with it? You haven't understood a thing.

SHE: What should I understand?

HE: Do you not care about what you've done?

SHE: What have I done?

HE: Look at me.

SHE: What am I supposed to see?

HE: Turn on the light, if you want.

SHE: What for?

HE: For you to understand better.

SHE: Understand what?

HE: If you saw my eyes, maybe they'd tell you.

SHE: You tell me.

HE: Put on the light.

SHE: There's no need.

HE: Put on the light.

SHE: Everyone's asleep. Do you want to wake them?

HE: No.

Pause.

SHE: We're fine like this.

HE: Try to understand. I'm asking you.

SHE: Not so loud.

HE: I'm begging you.

SHE: God, what? What are you begging me for? I don't understand.

HE: Does it have to be so obvious, so lewd, so coarse?

SHE: I don't know what you're talking about. You're always stringing me along, with your strange words. Why don't you just say what you mean and we can save all this... agonising?

HE: Does this matter to you?

SHE: Not enough to argue about.

HE: You know what I'm talking about.

Pause.

SHE: Yes. It matters.

HE: It matters. How much?

SHE: Does it matter to you? That's what I came to ask.

HE: That's not true. You came to talk about the men. That you'd gone out looking for them.

SHE: I didn't go out looking for anyone.

HE: You showed off in front of them, like a bitch in heat. Displaying your power, your power as a huntress, so you could come crowing back to me.

SHE: You're mad.

HE: And you've just realised? Why would that be?

SHE: I want to go.

HE: Yes, of course. Go.

SHE: You're not stopping me?

HE: No.

SHE: You don't need me?

HE: No.

Pause.

SHE: You're hurting me.

HE: I didn't touch you. Not this time.

SHE: That's the problem.

HE: Very vulgar.

SHE: Will I tell you a story?

HE: No.

SHE: The last one.

HE: You've forgotten the drink.

SHE: There'll be a drink tomorrow.

HE: There won't be a tomorrow.

SHE: The story…

HE: Do you hear that?

Pause.

It's raining again. There's no sense to anything. Things are important only because they seem important. They might not exist, they might not happen, and nothing changes. Time just wears us down. It finishes us.

SHE: It'll pass. It'll get better.

HE: No. Leave it. Just go.

SHE: Okay. I'll come back tomorrow.

HE: There won't be a tomorrow.

SHE: I'll come and look for you. You'll be here.

HE: I'll make sure I'm not.

SHE: You're frightening me.

HE: I don't believe that for a moment. Not now. Anyway, as I said, nothing matters that much. You're not worth the attention I'm paying you.

SHE: The story.

HE: I'm not interested.

SHE: It's very short.

HE: I said….

SHE: The woman felt lonely.

HE: Stand still.

HE draws close to her, breathes her in, caresses her with his look, desires her.

SHE: She went out of her cave.

HE: Why did she live in a cave – was she a woman or a fox? A vixen…

SHE: She lived in the dark. But one day she went out. The woman went out and they caught her. She was their prey. They hunted her down.

HE: Who?

SHE: They put their hands on her.

HE: Who?

SHE: They emptied themselves into her.

HE: Who?

SHE: But in the middle of the shadows she could see the face of another man. Even though she was their prey, she devoured them, thinking about another man.

HE pushes her away.

HE: I'm not interested. What were the rumours you came to tell me about?

SHE: Take care. People. They're searching.

8

SHE's standing behind him. HE's sitting on a chair, keeping his back to her as he gazes into space.

HE: 'I'm sick. And you expect me to smile through my misery. Don't you? Say something. Are you listening? Are you sure you're listening? It would be worth it just for once, for this one last time, if we could tell each other everything as it is, or as we think it is. Would it not? That's how I see it. No, no, stand still; please, this time it's absolutely critical that you breathe very gently, that you don't close your eyes, that you stay still. Just this once. There's no moon. We are truly alone. Exactly like then. When I was seven. She was twice my age. She was simple. I'm not being unkind, she really was, she used to drool and things like that. One of her eyes, I think it was the right one, used to wander towards the ceiling while she was looking at you with the other one. Her name was Rebecca. She had a beautiful name at least. You could see Rebecca was racked by desire. I did it out of kindness. It's no different now. I enjoy it more with you, but deep down it's always the same thing. That night there was no moon either. A coincidence, don't you think? There was nobody about. It was still early. Barely nine o'clock. Rebecca was on her own. She could feel my presence. She knew I was watching her. Her mother was shouting for her from the doorway. "Come on in, Rebecca, come on in." Rebecca paid no heed. She was just staring into space, in two different directions at the same time. Being Rebecca. Staring blankly down the dark alley, and at the descending darkness. It wasn't my childish appearance that made her notice me, it was my smell, the heavy breathing, the fact that my heart was pounding like some mad drummer. Just a couple of steps…I was standing in front of her. Her milky throat was crying out for me to bite her. She was smelly. A bad smell. I had this boiling feeling of malice, and I groped her under her skirt. Not her cunt. I wrapped my arm round her waist, and I ground the palm of my hand into her backside. Arse sounds better. The contact lasted barely five seconds or so, but you really could call it an eternity of the flesh. And then I kissed her, a clumsy hot naïve brutal kiss. Once, twice, three times while I groped around her buttocks. I could feel her breath coming in shorter bursts. I knew it was risky, that if anyone happened to glance our way, anyone at all, I would have been for it. I knew all right. But that feeling, that possibility, of stealing, of breaking in and taking something by force, of destroying somebody else in such a sweet way, it made me keep marauding around Rebecca's ridiculous tits and lumpy waist. And then I let her go. I ran, I stopped and I looked back. That vacant ugly leering face, her lips slightly apart, thick wet lips, they had the word 'desire', in all its full obscenity, written all over them, and they restored me to the night, to the idea that I'd taken something, that she would always remember it but that that was all there would ever be. I don't think anybody ever kissed her again. She was repulsive. I did it out of disdain, out of repugnance…for myself. You can do anything when you're a child. Fresh, firm flesh… The hunter game. Now there's just disgust. Flaccidity. Despair. Loneliness. The same perverse game, but less fun. Do you understand? It's no different now. It's exactly like then. Do you understand? Rebecca has a different name. Rebecca. You're Rebecca.'

Pause.

SHE: That's what you said to her?

HE: Yes.

SHE: And her name was Rebecca, like in the story.

HE: It's not a story. No. Her name wasn't Rebecca.

SHE: And what happened?

HE: She was crying.

SHE: And you?

HE: I sat and watched her cry.

SHE: But she wasn't Rebecca.

HE: No, I hardly knew her.

SHE: Did you love her?

HE: I wanted her.

SHE: What did she say, what did she do?

HE: Nothing. She threw herself into the river. So I heard.

9

The door is closed between them. HE refuses to appear until the end.

HE: Just take no for an answer.

SHE: It'll do you good.

HE: I'll be the judge of what'll do me good.

SHE: This will do you more good.

HE: I've no intention of finding out whether you're right or not.

SHE: I want to come in… Sorry. Would you mind opening the door, señor, please.

HE: I said no.

SHE: I've got your drink.

HE: I didn't order a drink.

SHE: It'll relax you.

HE: I don't think so. I feel worse than ever. My head's sore, I can't breathe and I feel like biting. Just stay away. And stop making so much noise. You'll wake everyone.

SHE: I don't care.

HE: Well I care. I need to sleep.

SHE: Then open the door.

HE: What good will that do?

SHE: We can talk, sort things out.

HE: What else is there to say? You've come out of this very well. I lost. Game over.

SHE: That's not true.

HE: Oh yes it is. I was the one dragged down. It was me who fell. I lost my balance. I haven't got much time left.

SHE: That's not true.

HE: I don't want to go on like this. I'm suffocating… I'm exhausted. Did you hear me? I was coughing my lungs up all afternoon.

SHE: You'll get better.

HE: I won't.

SHE: Have faith.

HE: Pigs have faith. What good does it do them?

SHE: Then have faith in me.

HE: You were right. You've got the better tools. You're much better made. Your machinery works. Your flesh is intact, in a manner of speaking. I don't know. I remember the story, the woman who was a fox who was hunted. You meant something by that, didn't you? I was at a disadvantage. I'm worn out. I ended up the weak one, the one that was dragged down, broken, ripped, exposed, run through. You have very subtle claws. But sharp.

SHE: I haven't done anything.

HE: That's right. I did it myself. I lurched into the mud myself. Into your mud.

SHE: What did I know? You taught me all these things.

HE: What did I teach you? Can you tell me?

SHE: No.

HE: Don't try to get out of it. You played and you played well. I knew you would.

SHE: You taught me how to enjoy it.

HE: Enjoy what?

SHE: This.

HE: What 'this'?

SHE: I don't know.

HE: A lot of useless words. Just shut up and go to bed. Go on. It's raining again.

SHE: It hurts.

HE: What hurts?

SHE: But I like it.

HE: I don't understand.

SHE: I like it hurting you.

HE: You don't know what you're saying.

SHE: That's what the game was.

HE: No. You don't understand any of it.

SHE: So what was it you wanted?

HE: I didn't want anything. I don't want anything. I don't know who you are. I don't know your name, I don't know what you're doing here. I'd like you to go now, or I'll call the manager.

SHE: Why are you doing this?

HE: I'm not doing anything.

SHE: There's something I have to tell you: I talked.

HE: I didn't expect anything different. It was foreseeable.

SHE: I told somebody. They know who you are.

HE: I don't know what you're talking about.

SHE: Are you saying you're not?

HE: I can't say anything about something I know nothing about.

SHE: I need to talk to you. Just talk. Please.

HE: What for?

SHE: I need to.

HE: You can talk to whoever you like. Your friends, the manager, the dog on the street. Just leave me alone.

SHE: No, you don't understand me. Why don't you want to understand me?

HE: What are you shouting for? It's night-time. Who are you looking for?

SHE: I need you.

HE: And I need to sleep.

SHE: I'm leaving.

HE: I don't blame you.

SHE: Do you care about me? Do you? Answer me. Do you?

HE: Lower your voice, please.

SHE: Tell me.

HE: …

SHE: Please…

HE: …

SHE: Think of the consequences.

HE: Are you threatening me?

SHE: Bastard.

HE: You are threatening me.

SHE: It'll be your fault.

HE: I don't know what's wrong with you, young lady.

SHE: Bastard…

> *SHE runs away. HE opens the door and emerges. HE talks to the audience as if they were fellow guests in the hotel.*

HE: What's going on? Because I have absolutely no idea. She was banging on my door. And then she ran off. She was talking about a river. We need to get help, because I couldn't make out what she was saying. I was too frightened to open the door. She said something about a river. And I was frightened…